DI032391

Treasure Hunters

TOMB EXPLORERS

NICOLA BARBER

Chicago, Illinois

Edited by Laura Knowles, Adam Miller, Harriet Milles, and Helen Cox Cannons
Designed by Victoria Allen
Original illustrations © Capstone Global Library Ltd 2013
Illustrated by Martin Bustamante
Picture research by Tracy Cummins

Originated by Capstone Global Library Ltd.
Production by Alison Parsons
Printed in the United States of America in North Mankato, MN. 082013 007670RP

16 15 14 13
10 9 8 7 6 5 4 3 2

Library of Congress Cataloging-in-Publication Data
Barber, Nicola.
 Tomb explorers / Nicola Barber.
  p. cm.—(Treasure hunters)
 Includes bibliographical references and index.
 ISBN 978-1-4109-4955-4 (hbk.)—ISBN 978-1-4109-4962-2 (pbk.) 1. Antiquities—Juvenile literature. 2. Archaeology—History—Juvenile literature. 3. Civilization, Ancient—Juvenile literature. 4. Tombs—Juvenile literature. 5. Treasure troves—Juvenile literature. I. Title.

CC171.B357 2013
930.1—dc23   2012012894

Acknowledgments
We would like to thank the following for permission to reproduce photographs:
Alamy pp.40, 41 (© Robert Harding Picture Library Ltd), 42 (Nathan Benn); Art Resources p.28 (©The Art Archive/British Library); Corbis pp.9 (©Bettmann), 19 (©Hulton-Deutsch Collection), 21 (©Robert Harding World Imagery), 35 (©Vanni Archive); ©Courtesy of the Penn Museum, image UR2327 p.13; Getty Images pp.6 (©DEA PICTURE LIBRARY/De Agostini). 8 (©De Agostini), 10 (©Universal History Archive), 14 (©Michael Melford), 15 (©AFP PHOTO/STR), 20 (©DEA/A. JEMOLO/De Agostini), 29 (©Chu Yong), 30 (©O. Louis Mazzatenta), 36 (©Ronaldo Schemidt/AFP); National Geographic Stock p.37 (©PEABODY MUSEUM OF HARVARD UNIV); newscom p.38 (©akg-images); Rex USA p.12 (©CSU Archv/Everett); Shutterstock pp.1 bot (©Vule), 1 top (©Potapov Alexander), 4 (©sisqopote), 5 (©Marco Tomasini), 7 (©Dudarev Mikhail), 16 (©Anthon Jackson), 17 (©Brian K.), 24 (©Jarno Gonzalez Zarraonandia), 26 (©Yan Vugenfirer), 27 (©Andre Viegas), 32 (©szefei), 34 (©Valery Shanin), 33 (©Wolverine1023), 39 top (©Tischenko Irina), 39 bot (©Ivancovlad), 43 (©Blaz Kure); Superstock pp.11 (©DeAgostini), 18 (©Fine Art Images), 25 (©age footstock). Design features: ©Shutterstock.

Cover photographs reproduced with permission of Shutterstock (©Pics-xl) and National Geographic Stock (©Kenneth Garrett).

Expert consultant
We would like to thank Dr. Michael Lewis for his invaluable help in the preparation of this book. Dr. Lewis is deputy head of the Department of Portable Antiquities and Treasure at the British Museum, London, England.

Guided Reading Level: V

CONTENTS

TOMBS AND TREASURE

Imagine you are a farmer, digging away in a field. Suddenly, you spot something in the ground beneath your feet--a hole, a glint of metal, an underground chamber. It's a one in a million chance, but it can happen!

Some of the most incredible tomb discoveries have been made by chance, and some have unearthed dazzling treasures. Others, of course, are the result of painstaking research and careful archaeological work. This book has examples of both kinds of discovery. Read on to find out more …

In Mexico during Day of the Dead celebrations, people make masks to remember their loved ones who have died.

In Petra, Jordan, these elaborate tombs were built high into the mountainside.

BURYING THE DEAD

From the very earliest times, people have wondered about what happens after death. Even today, the passing of a person from life to death is dealt with in many different ways around the world. Some people bury their dead in the ground or in tombs. Some prefer to cremate (burn) the dead body. These customs reflect the many different beliefs about life after death—the afterlife.

Everything but the kitchen sink?

In past times, people were often buried with the things they would need in the afterlife. Even the poorest people were sometimes buried with a cooking pot or other everyday object. In the tombs of wealthy or noble people, the objects considered necessary for the afterlife included:

- furniture
- weapons
- armor
- jewelry
- food.

TREASURE TROVES

Some of the tombs unearthed in the past have been full of spectacular treasures. The ancient Egyptian boy-king, Tutankhamun, was buried in a gold sarcophagus, and his tomb contained his golden throne, chariot, and countless other amazing objects. In the 1870s, excavations to find the tomb of the mythological Greek king Agamemnon unearthed a treasure trove of golden objects, including cups, swords, crowns—and a golden death mask.

This golden death mask was found at Mycenae, Greece, in 1876.

BOOBY TRAPS AND CURSES!

Over the centuries, despite the best attempts of the tomb-builders to stop them, thieves and robbers have plundered many tombs. In ancient Egypt, the builders of the great pyramids, where pharaohs (kings) were buried, tried lots of tricks to keep the robbers out.

Entrances into the Egyptian tombs were hidden and sealed. Inside there were secret passages, concealed doors, and dead ends. Razor-sharp wires, laid as traps across tunnels, were capable of slicing a thief's head off. If the robbers did get into the tomb itself, grim curses doomed them to terrible punishments in the afterlife. None of this seemed to stop their missions to steal, though!

Eye in the sky

Some places are difficult to explore on the ground. Lots of ancient remains are in hot deserts or in countries that are dangerous to visit. Using photographs taken from airplanes and satellite images, archaeologists can spot possible sites from marks and patterns on the ground that can only be seen from the sky. Of course, if they want to find out more, they still have to get to the site and explore further!

ROYAL TOMBS OF UR

It is some time around 2000 BCE. On the banks of the Euphrates River, in the region called Mesopotamia, stands a city made of mud bricks. Its name is Ur. Around it is rich and fertile farmland, watered by the great river. Flash forward 3,000 years. All that is left of Ur are a few ruins, surrounded by hot desert.

It was these ruins that brought British archaeologist Charles Leonard Woolley to Iraq in 1922. Woolley had permission to start excavations at the site of the ancient city. He and his team began digging in 1923. Little did they know that their work at the site was to continue for another 11 years ...

Mesopotamia, meaning "land between rivers," was the name given to the region between the Tigris and Euphrates rivers, which today lies mostly in Iraq.

GREAT ZIGGURAT OF UR

DIGGING STARTS

Woolley started excavating near the ruined Great Ziggurat (see the picture at left). His workers uncovered the ruins of ancient buildings, human burials, and precious jewelry. But by March, the desert was too hot for them to continue digging. Woolley went back to England, eager to return in the fall, when it would be cool enough for work to start again.

Leonard Woolley carefully brushes sand and earth off 4,000-year-old discoveries at Ur.

HUMAN SACRIFICE

Woolley eventually uncovered around 1,840 human bodies at Ur, including those in 17 royal tombs. He believed that some of the bodies were those of servants, who had been sacrificed (killed) and buried to care for their dead rulers in the afterlife.

ROYAL TOMBS

Over the next few years, Woolley unearthed the remains of houses and everyday objects that told him a lot about how the people of Ur (the Sumerians) lived. From 1926, Ur's "Royal Cemetery" was excavated, which revealed spectacular objects. These included a gold necklace decorated with precious stones, as well as a small wooden box beautifully decorated with shell and the blue gemstone lapis lazuli. Woolley and his team were amazed. They were sure these objects came from the tombs of kings and queens!

The little wooden box found by Woolley was covered with pictures of soldiers and their chariots.

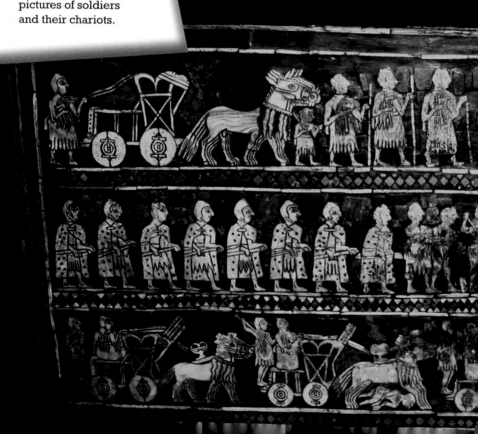

QUEEN PU-ABI

It was clear that some of the royal tombs at Ur had already been robbed of their treasures, but Woolley discovered one that lay undisturbed. The skeleton of Queen Pu-abi lay in a stone chamber, together with at least three of her servants.

The queen was surrounded by jewelry and other precious objects. There was no door into the tomb, so it seems that the dead queen was lowered down through the roof before being sealed in.

Next to Queen Pu-abi's tomb lay a "death pit" containing the remains of a chariot, oxen, and several more attendants.

This golden bull's head (below) once decorated a harp.

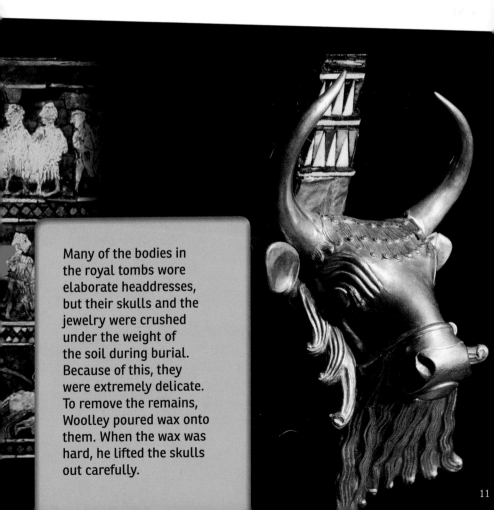

Many of the bodies in the royal tombs wore elaborate headdresses, but their skulls and the jewelry were crushed under the weight of the soil during burial. Because of this, they were extremely delicate. To remove the remains, Woolley poured wax onto them. When the wax was hard, he lifted the skulls out carefully.

THE TOMBS BECOME FAMOUS!

The excavations and finds at Ur were big news back in the United States and Europe. Woolley often wrote reports for the newspapers, and some people were so intrigued that they made the journey to Iraq to see the excavations for themselves. One of Woolley's guests was the famous writer of murder mysteries, Agatha Christie. She fell in love not only with the city but also, on her second visit, with Woolley's assistant, Max Mallowan. The two were married in 1930-- the same year they first met.

Agatha Christie wrote about her time at Ur. She described how she fell in love with the ancient city, and how seeing objects being carefully removed from the soil made her want to be an archaeologist.

LIFE ON SITE

Woolley and his wife, Katherine, spent 11 years living at Ur during the "excavation seasons"— October to March. Before any digging began, Woolley built an expedition house with living quarters, offices, and space to store objects from the dig. The house was a necessity because the weather in southern Iraq was often cold and wet during the winter months. Even so, the roof leaked, and there were few luxuries for its inhabitants.

Workers line one of the huge pits dug at Ur.

Skull secrets

Today, the human remains from the royal tombs are still revealing secrets. Modern scanning equipment used on two servants' skulls has revealed fractures caused by blows to the back of the head. Were these servants violently killed before being buried with their royal rulers?

THE PHARAOH'S TOMB

The year is about 1140 BCE. In the Valley of the Kings, on the west bank of the Nile River, teams of laborers are hard at work digging into the hillside. They are preparing a tomb for their pharaoh, Ramses VI.

As the workers tunnel into the rock, sweating in the hot sun, they bring out piles of rubble, which they use to construct rough shelters for themselves. They do not realize that they are building over the entrance to another small tomb.

This is how the tomb of the boy-pharaoh Tutankhamun was covered up and forgotten for thousands of years ...

JOURNEY TO THE NEXT WORLD

The ancient Egyptians believed firmly in life after death. Very wealthy people were buried in elaborate tombs with all the possessions they would need in the afterlife. But the Egyptians also believed that it was essential to preserve the dead body for its new life in the Next World. This process was called mummification.

This is Tutankhamun's death mask (see page 20).

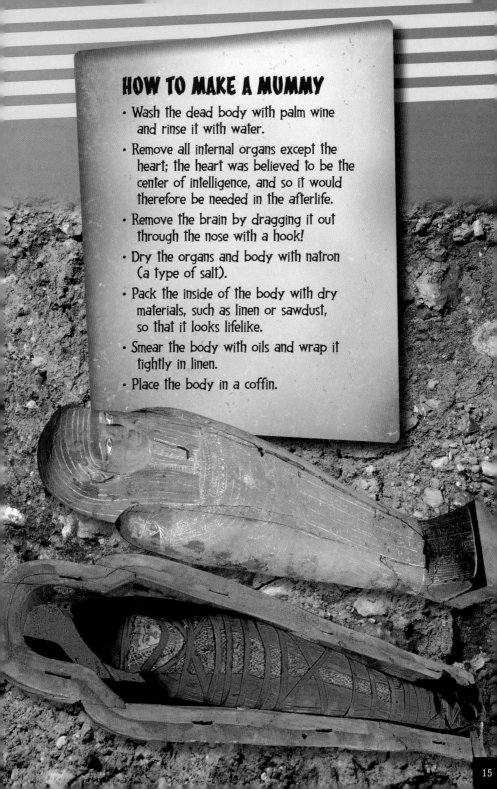

HOW TO MAKE A MUMMY

- Wash the dead body with palm wine and rinse it with water.
- Remove all internal organs except the heart; the heart was believed to be the center of intelligence, and so it would therefore be needed in the afterlife.
- Remove the brain by dragging it out through the nose with a hook!
- Dry the organs and body with natron (a type of salt).
- Pack the inside of the body with dry materials, such as linen or sawdust, so that it looks lifelike.
- Smear the body with oils and wrap it tightly in linen.
- Place the body in a coffin.

PYRAMIDS
AND TOMBS

The ancient Egyptian pharaohs spent huge amounts of time and labor building elaborate tombs for themselves. The early pharaohs were buried in huge stone pyramids. But these giant tombs attracted looters, so later pharaohs built their royal tombs in a remote valley near the city of Thebes—the Valley of the Kings.

The pharaohs' tombs were carved out of the rocky hillside, and many were completely hidden away, with no obvious entrance. But that did not stop the tomb robbers!

The Great Pyramid is the tomb of Pharaoh Khufu. It took over 20 years to build!

CARTER AND CARNARVON

By the 1920s, the royal tombs of the Valley of the Kings had become well known. But a British archaeologist named Howard Carter was convinced that there was one tomb that lay undiscovered—and clues suggested it could be that of a little-known pharaoh named Tutankhamun.

Carter's work was being paid for by a wealthy sponsor, the fifth Earl of Carnarvon. However, after years of searching with no result, Lord Carnarvon was running out of money and patience.

THE DISCOVERY

In November 1922, Carter decided to excavate one small triangle of ground that was still unexplored. After only three days, he made an amazing discovery— steps leading down to a sealed tomb! Carter checked that the seals were intact, then he re-covered the steps and sent a telegram to Lord Carnarvon in England.

"AT LAST HAVE MADE WONDERFUL DISCOVERY IN VALLEY. A MAGNIFICENT TOMB WITH SEALS INTACT. RE-COVERED SAME FOR YOUR ARRIVAL. CONGRATULATIONS."

CARTER'S TELEGRAM TO LORD CARNARVON ON THE DISCOVERY OF TUTANKHAMUN'S TOMB

THE GLINT OF GOLD

Work on the excavation restarted when Lord Carnarvon arrived. The first doorway opened on to a passage full of rubble. Carter and the others cleared the rubble away and came to a second doorway, covered in Tutankhamun's seals. What would they find on the other side? A looted chamber, or a treasure trove? Carefully, Carter made a small hole in the corner and peered in by the light of a candle.

"AS MY EYES GREW ACCUSTOMED TO THE LIGHT, DETAILS OF THE ROOM EMERGED SLOWLY FROM THE MIST, STRANGE ANIMALS, STATUES, AND GOLD— EVERYWHERE THE GLINT OF GOLD. FOR THE MOMENT—AN ETERNITY IT MUST HAVE SEEMED TO THE OTHERS STANDING BY— I WAS STRUCK DUMB WITH AMAZEMENT, AND WHEN LORD CARNARVON, UNABLE TO STAND IN SUSPENSE ANY LONGER, INQUIRED ANXIOUSLY, 'CAN YOU SEE ANYTHING?' IT WAS ALL I COULD DO TO GET OUT THE WORDS, 'YES, WONDERFUL THINGS.'"

HOWARD CARTER, DESCRIBING THE MOMENT HE LOOKED INSIDE THE TOMB FOR THE FIRST TIME

TUTANKHAMUN

- He was king of ancient Egypt around 1333–1323 BCE.

- He inherited the throne as a young boy.

- He was married to his half-sister, Ankhesenamun.

- He died unexpectedly at the age of about 18.

A CURSE?

A few weeks after the dramatic opening of Tutankhamun's tomb, Lord Carnarvon died from an infected mosquito bite. Rumors quickly spread that his death was the result of "Tutankhamun's curse"—a punishment for disturbing the young pharaoh's tomb after 3,000 years. Carter dismissed such stories as ridiculous, and he himself lived for another 16 years.

This shows the moment the tomb was opened.

THE BOY KING'S COFFIN

The room that Carter and Lord Carnarvon first glimpsed in November 1922 turned out to be an antechamber. It was filled with hundreds of objects that Tutankhamun was thought to need in the afterlife—beds, chariots, ointment jars, and games. It was not until February 1923 that Carter finally opened up the burial chamber.

Inside the burial chamber were three coffins shaped in the image of the pharaoh himself. Two were made from decorated wood, but the innermost one was solid gold! Placed directly over Tutankhamun's face was a magnificent death mask made from gold and decorated with colored glass and gemstones. It was simply breathtaking.

TREASURY TROVE

A small room off the burial chamber (known as the treasury) contained many more amazing objects, including Tutankhamun's internal organs! The organs were preserved in special alabaster containers called canopic jars (see below).

A sickly king

In recent years, new tests have revealed secrets about Tutankhamun's health and how he died. Using samples taken from Tutankhamun's mummified bones, scientists now know that the young pharaoh had a painful bone disease. This disease may have caused him to walk with a limp and use a cane. He probably also suffered from malaria.

The treasury contained some small, carved figures that probably symbolized workers who would serve the pharaoh in the afterlife.

It took 10 years of painstaking work for Carter's team to catalog and remove all the treasures from Tutankhamun's tomb.

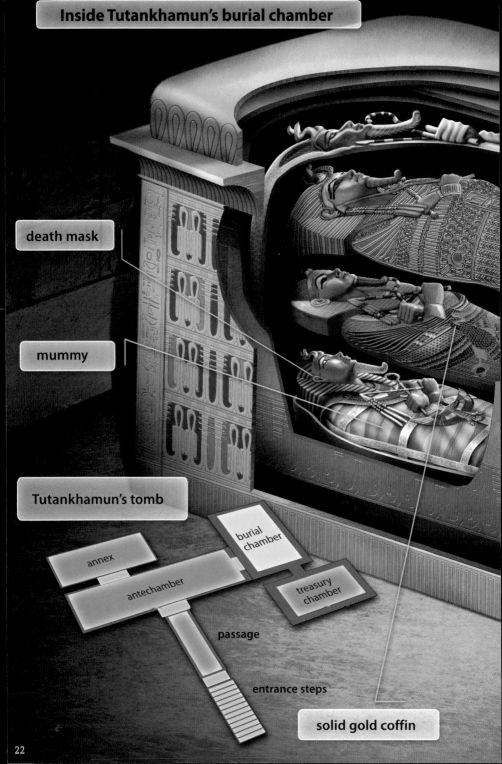

Inside Tutankhamun's burial chamber

death mask

mummy

Tutankhamun's tomb

annex

antechamber

burial chamber

treasury chamber

passage

entrance steps

solid gold coffin

22

2 wooden coffins

3 gold-covered, wooden shrines

stone sarcophagus

A TERRACOTTA ARMY

In spring 1974, three farmers from the Shaanxi province of China decided to dig a new well. The farmers lived on Mount Li (Lishan), close to the ancient tomb of the first emperor of China, Qin Shi Huangdi. People in that region were used to finding occasional bits and pieces of ancient pottery as they worked their fields. But as the farmers dug deeper, their shovels started to turn up parts of pottery figures--heads, arms, and legs--that were lifelike and life-size! They did not know it yet, but the farmers had made one of the most astonishing discoveries of all time.

THE EMPEROR'S ARMY

The farmers reported their amazing find, and very quickly excavations began. The results were stunning. An army of warriors made from terracotta (clay) lay buried in a huge underground pit. The warriors were all life-size, and they were arranged in battle formation, ready to defend the emperor's tomb from attack.

The pit discovered by the farmers turned out to be massive. It was 754 feet (230 meters) long by 207 feet (63 meters) wide, and it contained an army of around 6,000 figures! These figures included foot soldiers, archers, and cavalry (men with horses).

Three more large pits have since been discovered. In total, it is estimated that there were more than 8,000 figures, 500 horses, and 130 chariots in the pits! Much of the site remains unexcavated, waiting to be explored by archaeologists in the future.

RESTORING THE ARMY

The pits that house the terracotta warriors were originally covered with wooden ceilings, but these had long since collapsed, and the figures were buried in earth and rubble. Many of them were broken and crushed. The archaeologists worked carefully to restore the figures, chariots, and horses in the pits.

HOW DID THEY DO THAT?

The terracotta warriors were manufactured in workshops, using clay from Mount Li. The head, arms, legs, and body were made separately, then the figure was put together. Archaeologists figured out that the heads of the figures were made from eight different basic face molds. The craftsmen then scraped and kneaded the clay of each face to create the delicate features, hair bun, and hat of each warrior. Every one is a different individual.

COLORFUL WARRIORS

The warriors as we see them today are mostly a reddish-gray color, so you will have to use your imagination to picture them as they once were—painted in bright colors! A few figures have been unearthed that still have traces of their original colors (see the opposite page).

X-ray technology

Scientists have used X-ray technology to find out more about the paints on the terracotta warriors. One color, known as Chinese purple, is particularly interesting. At that time, most dyes for coloring clothes or making paints were simply extracted from plants or minerals. But Chinese purple was manufactured from various minerals, in a process that took many hours and required high temperatures. Now X-ray technology has allowed the scientists to identify exactly how this color was made.

THE FIRST EMPEROR

Who was Qin Shi Huangdi, and why did he need a terracotta army to guard his tomb? Ying Zheng became king of the state of Qin in ancient China in 246 BCE. At that time, Qin was one of seven rival states in China, all competing with each other for power. Ying Zheng ruthlessly set about taking over these states by war and by cunning. In 221 BCE, he declared himself emperor and took the name Qin Shi Huangdi.

QIN SHI HUANGDI

- Personal name: Ying Zheng

- He became king of the state of Qin at the age of 13.

- He declared himself Qin Shi Huangdi (First Sovereign Qin Emperor) in 221 BCE.

- He ordered the construction of a great wall to protect the northern borders of his empire.

- He had several huge palaces built. The largest had a reception hall that could hold 10,000 people!

SECRETS OF THE TOMB

One of the first things that Ying Zheng did as king of the state of Qin was to start work on his own tomb! Work began on a huge construction project that was to employ up to 700,000 workers for over 30 years. Historical records suggest that some of these workers were craftsmen, but most were prisoners, slaves, or people who needed to repay debts.

It is said that when the emperor died in 210 BCE, many of the craftsmen were killed and buried alongside him, so that no one could betray the secrets of what exactly lay inside the massive tomb.

This is the hill that covers Qin Shi Huangdi's tomb.

UNDERGROUND EMPIRE

Today, the tomb of Qin Shi Huangdi himself remains unopened. Experts are concerned that current technology is not advanced enough to protect the precious objects that may be inside the tomb. However, archaeologists have done enough excavations around the site to have a sense of its almost unbelievable size and scale.

The emperor built his tomb as a copy of his empire on Earth. This huge underground city included walls and gates, stables, and offices. Everything the emperor needed in life was replicated for his life after death, including entertainers and acrobats, bronze chariots, and even a zoo for exotic animals!

This body armor made from stone plates woven together with copper wire was found near Qin Shi Huangdi's tomb.

Around 100 years after the death of Qin Shi Huangdi, a Chinese historian named Sima Qian wrote a remarkable account of the emperor's tomb. He tells how workers built models of palaces and pavilions and filled the tomb with precious treasures. They even made constellations of stars on the ceilings, using pearls.

RIVERS OF MERCURY

Sima Qian tells of "rivers of mercury" inside the emperor's tomb, constructed to flow through the tomb like the great Yangtze and Yellow rivers. Could such a story be true? Amazingly, recent scientific work on samples taken from deep within the tomb confirm that there are indeed unusually high levels of mercury in the soil there.

Qin Shi Huangdi was determined that his tomb should not be disturbed. He ordered booby traps to be set up loaded with crossbows that would automatically fire if anyone dared to try to break in!

SECRETS IN THE RAIN FOREST

In the foothills of the Tumbalá mountains in eastern Mexico lies the ancient Maya city of Palenque. The ruins of the city are set on a ledge that overlooks swampy plains to the north, with mist–shrouded forest covering the mountains to the south and west. For many centuries after its decline, sometime around 800 CE, the city lay undisturbed and unknown to the outside world.

WHO WERE THE MAYA?

From as early as 1800 BCE, the Maya people settled across Central America. At their highest state of development, around 250 to 900 CE, they ruled over a large empire that included parts of present-day Mexico and El Salvador, as well as Belize and Guatemala. They developed a system of writing and built elaborate temples for the worship of their gods.

After 800 CE, the Maya civilization declined, and many of its cities became part of the jungle, including Palenque.

With little knowledge of the Maya civilization, many early Europeans who explored Palenque simply did not believe that Native Americans could have built such impressive buildings. They thought Palenque was the work of ancient Egyptians, Greeks, or Romans!

THE MYSTERIOUS CITY

From the early 1500s, various European explorers came across this mysterious city, buried deep in the jungle. The 20th century saw the arrival of archaeologists, eager to unravel its secrets.

One of these archaeologists was a Mexican named Alberto Ruz Lhuillier. In 1948, he decided to investigate some strange stone plugs in a flooring slab in one of the temples. What he found changed the world's view of the Maya forever.

ruins of Palenque

HOT WORK

The stone plugs noticed by Ruz Lhuillier covered holes in a slab on the floor of the Temple of Inscriptions—the largest of the Mayan stepped-pyramid structures. Lhuillier realized that something lay hidden beneath the floor—but what? It took four long years of digging to find out.

This is the Temple of Inscriptions.

Underneath the floor, Ruz Lhuillier and his team uncovered a staircase leading down into the depths of the temple-pyramid. The archaeologists could only excavate the site for a short time each year, from April to July—heavy rains made digging too dangerous for the rest of the time. It was hot, dark, and dusty work, as the staircase twisted and turned deeper and deeper beneath the temple.

THE PRIZE

As they dug down, the men had to remove large rocks that blocked their way. Were these deliberately put in place to protect whatever lay at the end of the tunnel? Finally, they came to the bottom of the staircase and to a wall. Behind it they found ornaments and painted shells—offerings left for gods.

A second wall led into a chamber that contained human bones. But the greatest prize was yet to come ... Punching a hole through another rubble wall, Ruz Lhuillier finally glimpsed a chamber that held a huge carved stone slab—a tomb.

"OUT OF THE DIM SHADOWS EMERGED A VISION FROM A FAIRY TALE ... IT SEEMED A HUGE MAGIC GROTTO CARVED OUT OF ICE, THE WALLS SPARKLING AND GLISTENING LIKE SNOW CRYSTALS."

RUZ LHUILLIER, DESCRIBING THE MOMENT OF DISCOVERY

PAKAL THE GREAT

Ruz Lhuillier had discovered the tomb of the Mayan ruler K'inich Janaab' Pakal the Great (603–683 CE), who ruled Palenque from the age of 12 until his death nearly 70 years later. During the last 10 years of his life, Pakal built the magnificent temple-pyramid for his burial.

Inside the burial chamber, Pakal's body was laid in a stone sarcophagus topped by a massive stone slab. The carvings on the stone slab show Pakal descending into the Mayan underworld (known as *Xibalba*)— the place of the dead.

JADE TREASURES

Inside the sarcophagus lay Pakal's skeleton wearing jade jewelry and surrounded by ornaments. These were placed on the body after death, and they included a jade collar made with beads, some in the shapes of flowers, and others like the heads of snakes. Pakal's fingers were adorned with jade rings. Most magnificent was Pakal's jade death mask, with eyes made from pieces of shell.

Pakal's death mask and collar are magnificent.

Remote-controlled discovery

Archaeologists have known about the existence of another tomb in Palenque since 1999, but have been unable to break into it for fear of the buildings above collapsing. In 2011, thanks to a tiny remote-controlled camera, the inside of the tomb was seen for the first time in 1,500 years. The camera was lowered in through a narrow shaft and revealed black figures painted on to a vivid blood-red background. Archaeologists believe this could be the tomb of the first ruler of Palenque, K'uk Bahlam I.

These are Mayan ruins at Palenque.

SHIP GRAVES

Throughout history, the wealthiest and most important people were often buried with everything they needed in the afterlife. The Vikings came originally from Scandinavia and were a great seafaring people. Among their most important possessions were their ships. So, maybe it's not surprising that Vikings of high rank were sometimes buried in or alongside their ships. Sometimes these were sent out to sea and burned.

ROTTEN LUCK!

Viking ships were made from wood, which rots away over time. But occasionally the conditions in the soil around the ship preserve the timbers. This is what happened in a grassy mound near Oseberg, in southern Norway. In 1903, a farmer named Knut Rom was digging into the mound when he came across the remains of ancient timbers.

The farmer contacted the University Museum of Oslo, and the following year an excavation team led by Professor Gabriel Gustafson started work. From the moment the digging began, it was clear that this was an exciting find ...

THE LAST JOURNEY?

The wet clay that enclosed the ship had preserved the wood remarkably well. Being very careful, Professor Gustafson and his team exposed the thousands of fragments of timber before removing them and preserving them. But there was no space in the Oslo University Museum for the restored ship. It was not until 1926 that the Viking ship made a perilous journey through the streets of Oslo and across the water to its new home, in the Viking Ship Museum at Bygdøy.

WHOSE GRAVE?

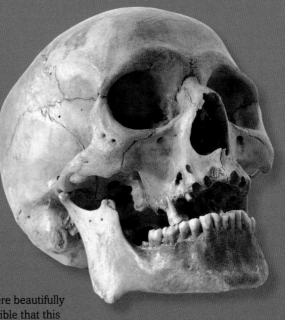

Who was buried in the Oseberg ship? Professor Gustafson found the remains of two women, one older and one younger, in a burial chamber at the back of the ship. The older woman was clearly of high rank, and she was buried with a great number of objects, including four wooden sleighs, a four-wheeled wooden cart, beds, kitchen tools, and an oil lamp.

Many of the wooden objects were beautifully carved and decorated. It is possible that this was the grave of the Viking queen Asa, and that her servant was sacrificed to care for her in the afterlife.

A NEW HOME?

The Oseberg ship may be on the move once again in the future. There are worries that this precious ship is slowly deteriorating because of the constantly changing amounts of moisture in the air in the present Viking Ship Museum. There are plans to move all the exhibits to a new museum with better facilities about 4 miles (6 kilometers) away. But would the fragile Oseberg ship survive another journey? This proposal has caused a lot of public debate in Norway.

So many people came to see the excavation that a fence had to be built to protect it and the delicate objects being found. Gustafson complained in his excavation diary that he himself was becoming an exhibit!

Less-wealthy Vikings were buried in ship-shaped graves marked out by stones.

MODERN REPLICA

Ever since the Oseberg ship was discovered, people have wondered what it would be like to sail it. In 1986–1987, a full-scale replica of the ship was built. But during its very first sailing tests in 1988, the ship capsized and sank!

A KEY TO THE PAST

The discovery of an ancient tomb does not just uncover gold and riches. It can also give us important information about people's lives in the distant past. Some of the most exciting recent finds have been in South America.

In 2011, archaeologists uncovered tomb sites in Peru that belonged to the Wari people. The Wari civilization flourished in the Andes mountains region between 600 and 1000 CE. In the tombs were gold bracelets, a silver mask, and a silver chest plate as well as silver-coated walking sticks and small models of cats. The archaeologists now hope that future finds will tell them a lot more about these little-known people.

"IT IS AN IMPRESSIVE WARI FIND IN THE CUZCO JUNGLE THAT OPENS A NEW CHAPTER ON ARCHAEOLOGICAL RESEARCH AND FORCES US TO RE-WRITE HISTORY..."

JUAN GARCIA, THE CULTURAL DIRECTOR FOR THE CUZCO REGION

Treasure from an ancient royal tomb in Peru, South America.

UNDISCOVERED SECRETS

Around the world, there are many ancient tombs that still lie shrouded in mystery. We may never know what is inside them, or who they belonged to, or why they were made. But it is possible that future technology may reveal more about such mysterious sites.

DO YOU HAVE WHAT IT TAKES?

You only have to read the stories in this book to know that finding a tomb requires a lot of dedication. It can take years of research, and then years more of hard work on the ground, and even then you might never find anything. You need to be fit, brave, and able to endure harsh conditions. Most of all, you need to be lucky!

Silbury Hill is the largest human-made hill in the United Kingdom, standing 131 feet (40 meters) high. Was it a tomb, or a giant sundial, or possibly an observatory to track the planets?

TIMELINE

4000s BCE
The Sumerians develop the earliest known civilization, in Mesopotamia.

2686-2181 BCE
This is the Old Kingdom period in Egypt and a time of pyramid-building.

c.2490-2340 BCE
This is the possible date for the construction of Silbury Hill in Britain.

c. 2000 BCE
This is the possible date for the construction of the ziggurat at Ur.

c. 1550-1069 BCE
This is the New Kingdom period in Egypt, when it is at the height of its powers.

1333-1323 BCE
Tutankhamun reigns in ancient Egypt.

246 BCE
Ying Zheng becomes king of the state of Qin.

221 BCE
Ying Zheng declares himself Qin Shi Huangdi (First Sovereign Qin Emperor), First Emperor of China.

210 BCE
Qin Shi Huangdi dies.

250-800 CE
The Mayan Empire is at its height.

c. 600-1000 CE
The Wari civilization flourishes in the Andes.

603-683 CE
The Mayan ruler Pakal the Great reigns in Palenque.

c. 800 CE
Palenque and many other Mayan cities are abandoned.

1876
Heinrich Schliemann excavates the tomb of Agamemnon in Mycenae.

1903
The Oseberg ship burial is discovered in Norway.

1922-1923
Howard Carter discovers Tutankhamun's tomb in Egypt.

1923
Charles Leonard Woolley starts excavations at Ur.

1926
The Oseberg ship is moved to the Viking Ship Museum in Oslo, Norway.

1932
Howard Carter and his assistants finish removing and cataloging objects from Tutankhamun's tomb.

1948
Alberto Ruz Lhuillier starts excavations in the Temple of Inscriptions in Palenque.

1974
Farmers in the Shaanxi province of China uncover a terracotta army.

Wari tombs are uncovered near Cuzco, Peru.

GLOSSARY

afterlife life after death

alabaster type of hard, white rock

antechamber smaller room next to a larger one, often used as an entrance

archaeologist scientist who specializes in archaeology

archaeology study of human history by examining remains and ruins such as burial sites and ancient cities

cavalry soldiers who are mounted on horses

death mask mask that is made from a mold taken from the face of a dead person, then used to cover the person's face

excavation archaeological dig

jade gemstone that is a bluish-green color

lapis lazuli gemstone prized for its intense blue color

loot stolen goods

mercury silver metal that is liquid in normal conditions

Mesopotamia "land between two rivers"—the ancient name for the region between the Tigris and Euphrates rivers that today lies mostly in Iraq

mummification ancient Egyptian method of preserving a dead body by removing the internal organs, drying and stuffing the body, and wrapping it in linen bandages

pharaoh title given to a king of ancient Egypt

sarcophagus stone coffin

satellite object that is placed in orbit around Earth by humans

scanning equipment type of equipment that is used to inspect something quickly and systematically

seal symbol used as a kind of signature—for example, on wax or on paper

sponsor someone who supports an event or an activity by providing money

tomb grave or burial place

ziggurat large pyramid-shaped tomb built in ancient Mesopotamia

FIND OUT MORE

BOOKS

Baquedano, Elizabeth. *Aztec, Inca and Maya* (Eyewitness). New York: Dorling Kindersley, 2005.

Gogerly, Liz. *Ancient Egypt* (Time Travel Guides). Chicago: Raintree, 2008.

Hart, George. *Ancient Egypt* (Eyewitness). New York: Dorling Kindersley, 2008.

Kops, Deborah. *Palenque* (Unearthing Ancient Worlds). Minneapolis, Minn.: Twenty-First Century, 2008.

Malam, John. *Lost and Found: The Terracotta Army and Other Lost Treasures.* Irvine, Calif.: QEB, 2011.

Margeson, Sue M. *Viking* (Eyewitness). New York: Dorling Kindersley, 2000.

WEB SITES

www.khm.uio.no/utstilling/faste/vikingskipene/index_eng.html
The Viking Ship Museum offers information about the Oseberg ship.

ngm.nationalgeographic.com/ngm/tut/mysteries
Visit this interactive National Geographic web site to learn more about Tutankhamun's tomb. A special feature allows you to examine his body up close.

www.penn.museum/sites/iraq
Read lots of fascinating information about the excavations at Ur.

www.travelchinaguide.com/attraction/shaanxi/xian/ terra_cotta_army/qin_shihuang_1.htm
The China Guide web site has lots of information about Qin Shi Huangdi, his tomb, and the terracotta army.

whc.unesco.org/en/list/411
Read the United Nations Educational, Scientific and Cultural Organization (UNESCO) description of the excavations at Palenque.

whc.unesco.org/en/list/441
The UNESCO web site has an excellent description of the terracotta army.

Places to visit

The American Museum of Natural History
Central Park West at 79th Street
New York, New York 10024-5192
www.amnh.org
The American Museum of Natural History
is home to many of the world's greatest
historical treasures. The museum contains
artifacts from many of the civilizations
explored in this book.

Smithsonian National Museum of
Natural History
10th Street and Constitution Avenue,
NW Washington, D.C. 20560
www.mnh.si.edu
The National Museum of Natural
History has archaeological finds
from many of the civilizations
mentioned in this book and more.

The Field Museum
1400 S. Lake Shore Drive
Chicago, Illinois 60605-2496
fieldmuseum.org
The Field Museum has an impressive
collection of artifacts, including many
from the cultures of the Americas.

Topics for further research

- See if you can find out more about some of the latest tomb finds in the
  Americas. New discoveries are being found all the time. In 2010, archaeologists
  found a 2,700-year-old pyramid in southern Mexico. It is believed to be the
  oldest tomb of its kind in Mesoamerica.

- Find out about some other Viking ship burials. For example, try to find
  information about the Skuldelev ships in Denmark. Check out the web site
  of the Danish Viking Ship Museum for lots of information about the
  Skuldelev ships: www.vikingeskibsmuseet.dk/en/.

- Learn more about the Valley of the Kings, where Tutankhamun's tomb was
  discovered. There are more than 60 tombs carved into the stone walls of
  the valley, and there may be many more that are still undiscovered.

INDEX